"Anyone who has known and read Scott Owens' prolific the past fifteen years is also aware that he takes his role as an artist and his place as a community activist seriously. This important collection finds him doing no less. While *Sky Full of Stars and Dreaming* is clearly set in the pandemic year just past, with its references to our "new normal," Owens focuses his heart and eye instead on the connections to nature and family and work that provide the gravity to not just hold him in this world, but to carry hope into that endeavor." —Tim Peeler, Author of *The Life and Times of Jaysus Christopher Duende and Darrel Cobb Runkle*

"In *Sky Full of Stars and Dreaming*, Scott Owens shares a world filled with life and possibility (even during a pandemic). This living world contains natural wonders making 'a sound as big as day' and the wonders of human relationships. Owens reminds us that even during our greatest moments of challenge we're still surrounded by hope, beauty, and so much life." —Robert Lee Brewer, Senior Editor, *Writers' Market*

"*Sky Full of Stars and Dreaming* is Scott Owens' newest collection, and with over a dozen books to his credit, Owens, a masterful poet, once again delivers poems that amaze, move, and delight a reader with their musicality, images, and depth. In his poem "Stack Rock Creek" he not only creates a lovely *ars poetica*, but also reveals a larger truth of how to live a life, a way of being in the world that is deeply embodied. In the poem, he writes, "a purpose, making/things stand/still/if only a moment/to be seen better." Owens' poems pause everyday moments and a wide range of life experiences for the reader to see more fully. These poems celebrate survivors and inspire a gratitude for the ability to not only survive but to thrive. His poems sing of a life well-lived and well-observed, and I will return to be in their good company often." —Malaika King Albrecht, President, NC Poetry Society

Other books from Redhawk Publications:

All I Wanted by Jake Young

Birdhouse by Clayton Joe Young and Tim Peeler

Bouquets Hadn't Been Invented Yet by Tony Deal

Food Culture Recipes from the Henry River Mill Village

From Darkness: The Fated Soules Series, Book One by Jan Lindie

Going To Wings by Sandra Worsham

The Hickory Furniture Mart: A Landmark History by G. Leroy Lail and Richard Eller

Hickory: Then & Now by Richard Eller and Tammy Panther

Hickory: Then & Now The Complete Texts by Richard Eller

Hickory: Then & Now The Complete Photograph Collection

Hurdles by Ric Vandett

The Legends of Harper House - The Shuler Era by Richard Eller *More* by Shelby Stephenson

Mother Lover Child & Me by Erin Anthony

Newton: Then & Now by Richard Eller and Sylvia Kidd Ray

Piedmont The Jazz Rat Of Cunningham Park by Mike Bruner

A Place Where Trees had Names by Les Brown

Polio, Pitchforks & Perseverance by Richard Eller

Sanctuary Art Journal 2018, 2019, 2020

Secrets I'm Dying to Tell You by Terry Barr

Sittin' In with the Sun by Carter Monroe

Sleeping Through the Graveyard Shift by Al Maginnes

Waffle House Blues by Carter Monroe

We Might As Well Eat by Terry Barr

We See What We Want to See:

The Henry River Mill Village in Poetry, Photography, and History by Clayton Joe Young and Tim Peeler

What Came to Me—Collected Columns Volume One by Arlene Neal

Win/Win by G. Leroy Lail

SKY
FULL
OF
STARS
AND
DREAMING

POEMS

SCOTT OWENS

REDHAWK
PUBLICATIONS

Redhawk Publications
2550 US Hwy 70 SE
Hickory NC 28602

Robert Canipe, Publisher and Editor rcanipe@cvcc.edu
Tim Peeler, Editor
Patty Thompson, Projects Director

ISBN: 978-1-952485-22-0

CONTENTS

SKY FULL OF STARS

Around...13
[Night sky full of stars]...14
Filling the Void...15
Cicada...16
In the Cathedral of Fallen Trees...17
Subterranean...19
Pansies...20
November...21
Looking Down the Ski Jump at Innsbruck...22
Passover in the Time of Pandemic...23
How to Enjoy a Spring Day...24
Yellow Xterra...26
12 Haiku...27
Stack Rock Creek...30
Adding Up the Day...32

WORDS AND WHAT THEY SAY

A Marriage...35
Miles to Go...36
I Teach My Daughter the Joy of Sound...37
[honeysuckle smell]...38
Family Outing...39
[the origami]...40
Cleaning During Covid...41
Clue...44

Six seniors sit at a table45
Father and Son...46
Words and What They Say...48

ONE HAND ON THE WHEEL

How I Got Here...50
Made to Be Broken...53
The Idea of Order at Soul's Harbor...54
Who Hasn't Contemplated Civil Disobedience Stuck Behind a
        Tractor Trailer Carrying Chickens to Dobson, NC...57
Everything Is Made...59
Teaching During the Pandemic...60
Small Talk...63
The Possibility of Substance Beyond Reflection...65
What Words Are Worth...66
Last...67
Survivors...69
A Lot About Limas...71
Something Better...74
Assurances...75

LONG YELLOW

Long Yellow...79
Utilitarian...80
Poem for This Saturday's Apocalypse...81
The Persistent Desire to Rise...82
[morning mirror]...83

Aubade...84
Sharing a Drink on My 55th Birthday...86
Isn't...87
Maybe This...88
Keeping Pace...89
Making Amends...90
Not Going Gently...91
Resistance...92
Only One...93
Just...94

ACKNOWLEDGMENTS

Grateful acknowledgement is due the following journals and anthologies where many of these poems were previously published:

Blue Pitcher for "Looking Down the Ski Jump at Innsbruck"

Blue Unicorn for "In the Cathedral of Fallen Trees"

Branches for "The Persistent Desire to Rise"

Chrysanthemum for [as if the green]

Crucible for "Adding Up the Day"

Innisfree Poetry Journal for "Resistance"

Lilipoh for "Words and What They Say"

notes from the gean for [morning mirror]

Pembroke for "Subterranean"

Pirene's Fountain for "In the Cathedral of Fallen Trees", [smooth stones]

Pinesong (NC Poetry Society) for [after dawn], Haiku Award, and "Keeping Pace" (Poetry of Love Award)

Red Dirt for "Who Hasn't Contemplated Civil Disobedience Stuck Behind a Tractor Trailer Carrying Chickens to Dobson, NC"

Rusty Truck for "Yellow Xterra"

vox poetica for "Keeping Pace," "Long Yellow" and "The Possibility of Substance Beyond Reflection"

Waterways for "Making Amends"

Willows Wept Review for [last leaf]

Word Salad for [mangrove labyrinth]

Your Daily Poem for "Pansies" and "Poem for This Saturday's Apocalypse"

"Adding Up the Day" was also previously published in the Poetry Society of SC Award Anthology (Gertrude Munzenmaier Award)

"In the Cathedral of Fallen Trees" was also previously published in *The Persistence of Faith* (Sandstone, 1994) and *Something Knows the Moment* (Main Street Rag, 2011)

[last leaf] was also previously published in the NC Haiku Society Anthology (2014)

"Long Yellow" was also previously published in *Thinking About the Next Big Bang in the Galaxy at the Edge of Town"* (Main Street Rag, 2015)

"Resistance" was also previously published in *Something Knows the Moment* (Main Street Rag, 2011)

"Who Hasn't Contemplated Civil Disobedience Stuck Behind a Tractor Trailer Carrying Chickens to Dobson, NC" was also previously published in *The Best of Poetry Lincolnton* and *Thinking About the Next Big Bang in the Galaxy at the Edge of Town"* (Main Street Rag, 2015)

SKY
FULL
OF
STARS

Around
after Caspar David Friedrich's *Monk at the Sea*

80% is sky
10 dark water
Alien and empty
Or unknown
All but one figure of the rest
Sand devoid of life

And yet he still stands
Solitary and small
As if he could matter
As if he could penetrate
Sky, water, earth
And understand

Night sky full of stars
dreaming in a lonely place –
whippoorwill

Filling the Void

They split the light
that filters in
through empty panes,
stretching shadows
longer than tails
across the page
I'm reading or the wall
I'm staring at
unable to fathom
its depth, or just
the empty air,
filled at last
with some shade of life.

Cicada

Not humming or vibrating or buzzing even,
words too small to convey
a sound as big as day.

Strident, ceaseless, maddening,
compression of something called
tymbals, a deforming of the body
as if your ribs collapsed
one at a time and sprang back
300 times a second
causing, maybe a scream,
not from a vocal cord
but from the body itself.

All this to attract a mate
frighten a competitor,
widespread as heat or haze
all defining traits
of Southern summer days.

In the Cathedral of Fallen Trees

Each time he thinks something special
will happen, he'll see the sky resting
on bent backs of trees, he'll find
the wind hiding in hands of leaves,

he'll read some secret love scratched
in the skin of a tree just fallen.
Because he found that trees were not
forever, that even trees he knew

grew recklessly towards falling,
he gave in to wisteria's plan
to glorify the dead. He sat down
beneath the arches of limbs reaching

over him, felt the light spread
through stained glass windows of leaves,
saw every stump as a silent altar,
each branch a pulpit's tongue.

He did not expect the hawk to be here.
He had no design to find the meaning
of wild ginger, to see leaves soaked
with slime trails of things just past.

He thought only to listen
to the persistent breathing of trees,
to quiet whispers of leaves in wind,
secrets written in storied rings.

Each time he thinks something special
will happen. He returns with a handful
of dirt, a stone shaped like a bowl,
a small tree once rootbound against a larger.

Subterranean

Beneath the leaves
      the mole
blind and bulled-shaped
tunnels into dark corners
travelling by touch
swimming with out-turned
hands through rooted earth
over rockshelf and nests
of crawling insects
stopping only to evade
unremembered fenceposts
or cross driveways
on padded feet.

He leaves his tracks
across the flower bed
      not of feet
but the print of his back
raising like Atlas
the earth on his shoulders
forging a labyrinthine
home in the dark world
of bright bulbs and sweet seeds
turning and reshaping the soil
visible only in sound
the quiet ripple
just below the surface.

Pansies

One has to wonder where they got
their reputation for pansiness.
Purple and proud, or any color
you might imagine, they grow
where they want to grow, despite the cold,
so much unlike their flashy cousins,
impatiens, petunias, scarlet sage,
petals falling off at first frost,
hardly hearty at all.
Keep your prima donna blossoms,
loud and boastful annuals, brief
and seedless. I'll take the pansies
of the world, unassuming, resilient,
quietly doing what they know to do.

November

Not a season exactly,
neither winter nor fall,
but something somehow
in between. This tree,
bereft of leaves
but left with these
dangling seedpods,
is like November,
unsettled, incomplete,
defoliated, depleted
but decidedly unbare,
like all of us,
always aging,
but never quite there.

Looking Down the Ski Jump at Innsbruck

The flier sees
not the long rows
of ancient stones
covered with moss
and graveyard poetry,
or the iron fence
rising spearlike
between the graves
and the yellow hospital,
or even the ring of faces
lifted upward
to follow his fractured flight
ripping through solid air,

but only the sea of blue
stretching out before him
and the one white wave
rushing up to catch him.

Passover in the Time of Pandemic

The white birch across the street
doesn't know, and sends up leaves as if
like every other spring it is time to grow.

And the coral bells in front of the house
don't know, stretching thin stems
of pink against the gray of another day.

And the song birds don't know,
sparrows and juncos spilling out
tiny bits of possibility.

Not even spring itself can know
what a challenge it is to rise
each day, how we struggle to find

what to do next, wonder if it's all
worth it, how we hold our breath
fearing that death might find its way

to our door and see the lintel unmarked.

How to Enjoy a Spring Day

Go outside, of course.
How could you not?
With the sun shining
on the other side
of still bare trees
making the sky seem
less far away, less
part of something
you never could attain.
Look, of course.
How could you not?
At the just starting
to appear tips of crocuses
pushing their way
through barely green grass,
at leafbuds on limbs,
almost ready to pop
open to warmth and rain.
Listen, of course.
How could you not?
To wind blowing
through limbs
across a sky
you've imagined would look
exactly the way it does.
Stop, lie down, rest.
How could you not?
You've made it again
and the whole world

seems willing
to take you in.
Mostly, breathe.
How could you not?

Yellow Xterra

With the rear seat folded up
he could just fit stretched out
in the back of the yellow Xterra,
but he was exceedingly happy that
with the rear seat folded up
he could just fit stretched out
in the back of the yellow Xterra.

Through tinted glass he saw
a perfect sky of stars,
broken only by shapes of leaves,
knew the quiet of solitude,
absence of expectation.

12 Haiku

Misty gray morning --
the world unfolds almost
as large as the sky.

after dawn a moment
of stillness -- everything
catches its breath

as if the green
might not be enough, a field
of purple flowers

intricate
spider's web –
my own eyes trapped

summer's bright red
what poppies know
of sin

storm clouds shatter
when we reach the river --
how wise old wives

mangrove labyrinth
of root and limb repairing
above and below

smooth stones
skipping across the lake--
receding voices

one
by one
the stars

last leaf hanging
in full moon -- black boat adrift
on silver lake

December morning
sky appears through stained glass
window of trees

wheelbarrow
filled with snow
so much is waiting

Stack Rock Creek

One has to wonder
how they got there,
what hands placed them
one atop another
just so to create
a wall in water
or several walls
that also create
ledge after ledge
and pools gathering
behind them until
the water spilled
over, cascading
into the next
pool below,
whether it could
possibly be
a single pair
of hands, a single
day or year,
and whether
they had to be
worked and reworked
as the water changed,
as the hands changed,
as the things carried
by the water, sometimes
displacing them, sometimes

making them disappear
altogether, changed,
whether it served
a purpose, making
things stand
still
if only a moment
to be seen better,
gathering, collecting,
saving for reflection,
or use, or merely
the possibility
of appreciation.

Adding Up the Day

This morning the sky was black
as earth. Today the ground stayed
wet all day. Today each leaf showed
a different shade of green.

I made a catalog of flowers,
a list of everything in bloom:
tame white pitchers of obedient plant,
loosestrife's purple chaos,
columbine's cluster of doves,
bright shining of moonbeam coreopsis,
fallen fingers of hibiscus.

If I were a flower my name
would be Ivy, the one
that grows beyond control.

I drink the air before me,
suck where the bee sucks,
leave nothing untongued.

I say to myself
the world is flowers
after all
if you want it to be
you make it that way
around you
and say
the world is flowers
after all.

WORDS

AND
WHAT
THEY
SAY

A Marriage

We work together, you and I.
You with your tireless planning.
I with my tireless doing.
We build, plant, grow, design,
cook, clean, teach.

We, you and I, work together.
Make the bed, make the coffee,
make things better, make time
for talking, listening, feeling,
being, becoming, loving.

You and I, we work together.

Miles to Go

A promise is a would-be bridge
made of finer stuff than spiders' webs,
whisper in a lover's ear,
sleeping baby's face,
bright, unconcealing glass.

Promises are never empty.
Promises are always full
of intention to reach across
the gulf that stretches between us.

Every conception is a promise,
every birth, every hand held,
every word, every pot set to boil.
Who makes no promises,
knows no love.

I Teach My Daughter the Joy of Sound

Philomena, she says from the back seat,
a name she's heard but not understood.
I play the game we've played before,
Filibuster? I ask. *No, Philomena*, she says again.

Do you mean *Filibustered Mustard?* I ask,
and hearing her laugh, I know.
Filibustered Mustard who only eats custard?
And the laugh comes again, and I know.

Filibustered Mustard who only eats custard
and always gets flustered? and again the laugh,
and then the hand on my arm, and I know in a way
that only such moments make clear, I'm in the right place.

honeysuckle smell --
my daughter comes in
from eating summer

Family Outing

My daughter digs up worms
from the old garden and moves them
one at a time to the new one,
her love of animals clear
in the way she carefully cradles
each one in a bare hand
letting the worm squirm
wherever it will across
her palm, keeping the other
hand below to catch it
should it go too far in any direction.
My wife plans, plots,
decides, directs number,
width, depth, selection.
I dig, set in place,
carry water. Together
we make again a garden
to tend, grow, sustain
us.

the origami
my daughter made --
wings unfurling

Cleaning During Covid

We start in the attic,
carry out 17 years of kept
but no longer used paraphernalia,
dishes and toys, decorations,
baby gates, six single beds,
the witch's cauldron we always swore
we'd make something out of.
Give what's wanted
to grown up children, friends,
donate most of the rest,
leave a pile by the road
for anyone else who'll take it.

Then we scrape the banged up
doorway from living room
to kitchen, repaint,
assemble a rack for shoes
behind the door, change
batteries and light bulbs,
fix the AC,
clean out the dryer hose,
sort through all the things
that haven't made it
to the attic yet.

Next, we move outside,
pressure wash patio,
driveway, sidewalk,
promise the house we'll come back,
clear the gutters,
trim trees, pull up weeds
we've ignored,
aerate and reseed
the lawn, move
volunteers from against the house
to places they might actually grow.

Finally, we descend
on the basement,
drag out tables
with rotted legs,
boxes for things we've kept,
pour out produce
we put by five years ago,
make a puddle of tomatoes,
jalapenos, pickles,
pepper jelly just far
enough away that the dogs
can't get into it,
sanitize the jars,
pack them back in boxes
for the next abundant harvest.

No vacation,
no trips anywhere,
no new projects that bring
people into our home.
This year the project
that keeps us together
is cleaning, doing all the things
we'd kept putting off,
making the most
of what we have and waiting
for better days to come back.

Clue

It always seemed to me they'd left the most important part out.
Sure the who was important, Mustard, Scarlet, Plum,
all the suspicious colors. And the where was of course where
discovery started, in the library, conservatory, study.
And the tool of choice determined just how immaculate
or macabre the act was. We imagined being bludgeoned
with a candlestick, wrench, or lead pipe, strangled
with a rope, bled out with a knife, or felled on our knees
execution style, the revolver still trembling in a thin hand
or fired a second, third, even fourth time into an inert body,
and that's where what's missing is made clear,
and, yes, I mean the detail, just a wrench was never enough.
Was it a small household Crescent wrench you might find
in any kitchen drawer or a red handled pipe wrench
like only Miss White's husband the plumber would have?
Was the knife a butcher knife, switchblade, or hunting knife
like Colonel Mustard kept beneath the driver's seat of his Austin Healey?
But also, and more so, I mean the motive.
Mr. Green consumed with jealousy, Scarlet set on revenge,
Plum afraid his indiscretions would be revealed
White driven mad with boredom, with loneliness,
with having nothing of interest to offer but this?
Mustard in yet another fit of rage?
And then not even a poet could say
why Mrs. Peacock liked the sound of the lead pipe
cracking through one skull after another on every family game night.

Six seniors sit at a table

at a local diner, 2 black, 4 white.
Good Christians all, they mention church
and the preacher every few sentences.
After basketball and grandchildren they mourn
the recent loss of a husband and wife nearby,
shot in a break-in defending home and possessions.
And then they mourn the circumstance
that leads to such desperation.

Sometimes things take my breath away,
like looking up through yellow gingko leaves.
They remind me how tenuous all judgment must be.
I do not share their faith, have more often
had reason to rail against their kind,
but some days my heart overflows with hope.

Father and Son

I see my son and wonder,
his hair in a blue bandana,
will the world permit him his happiness.
Good morning, he always
seemed to say, *today,*
will be a wonderful day.
Something good is going to happen,
and he would skip along his way.

Today, those I see around him
don't understand his happiness,
although they are drawn to it,
his hair in a blue bandana,
as an oddity, as taboo,
as something like addiction.

Others rise up against it.
The realists, pragmatists,
gatekeepers of society,
they find him dangerous,
and they would like to change him.
They want to show him
the impossibility of such levity.
They want to make him,
his hair in a blue bandana,
more like them,
eyebrows knitted together,
mouth closed in a serious expression.

I see my son,
his hair in a blue bandana,
and I wonder how he stays
the way he is, and why
I never had the strength he has.
I walk over to him
and give him a hug
and lean in close
to whisper in his ear,
I love the blue bandana.

Words and What They Say

Some say you can't tell anything
from the language that people use,
that Eskimos in fact have no
more words for snow than we,
nor Anglo-Saxons more
for cut, stab, thrust,
and the fact that our words for animals
when we eat them, *beef, pork,*
poultry, all come from French
doesn't prove they're better
cooks or bigger carnivores,
any more than 23 acronyms
for laughter shows that texting
teens just want to have fun,
but when I hear my carful of 2nd graders
from Sandy Ford Montessori School
making up names for the sun,
and the moon, and the stars that only
come out when you're camping and the fire
goes out, and you turn off your flashlights
while your mother holds you in her arms,
I can't help but believe
that not only is there hope for us all
but that the hope we have
grows stronger
when we can put it into words.

ONE
HAND

ON

THE

WHEEL

How I Got Here

I got here by the word of God
according to my grandmother who told
my mother she ought to get married
because she was bound to sin if she didn't.
I got here by two people too young
to know what they ought not to do,
seventeen year old boy thinking
he couldn't live without a fourteen year old girl.
I got here by luck or bad luck
of the draw, in a rage of teenage
hormones, libido gone wild.
I should have been unplanned, but I wasn't.
I got here by having belt buckles
lashed across legs, hands
burned on electric stoves,
by being locked in closets for hours.
I got here by running away
more times than I can count
only to go home the next day.
I got here by being called stupid.
I got here by riding the book mobile
in its great circle around Greenwood
County so I could read
more books than I could check out.
I got here by asking for a job
when I was eight and getting it
and working every day of my life since then.

I got here by being shoved
into the back wall of a baseball dugout
by my own father and shoving back,
by never backing down from anyone
wanting to be called *Daddy*.
I got here by walking down
one hill and up another
until I found myself
fourteen miles from home,
by traveling with other people's
families when mine went nowhere,
by leaving at seventeen,
riding the Greyhound bus
from Greenwood to Athens, sleeping
on couches and backseats of cars
instead of ever going back.
I got here by coming to a state
that values education
lower than forty-eight others.
I got here by convincing more
than one woman that I might be
worth the effort after all.
I got here by driving late night
roads, looking for answers
in reflections of headlights on asphalt.
I got here on the wings of dreams
and schemes and other things
refusing to be kept in boxes.
I got here by believing it matters
to try to make a difference.
I got here by writing poems

that nobody gives a damn about
but writing them anyway,
by writing this poem
and giving it to you thinking
you might care where you get to.

Made to Be Broken

Only sometimes it was about skill,
walking on the railhead
without tipping from side to side.

Only sometimes it was about courage,
climbing hand over hand
to the very tops of trees.

Of course sometimes it was merely showing off,
jumping the widest part of the creek
despite the bridge nearby.

But always it was about pushing the rules
of childhood to learn how and how far
you could push the boundaries of life.

The Idea of Order at Soul's Harbor

No one can say exactly where
it begins. The sources alone
seem endless, too many mountain
streams, too many highlands
where creeks are divided east
or west by some random crest
and what falls, further down, converges.

Everything flows downhill
from places without names
above Caesar's Head, Raven Cliff,
Persimmon Ridge,
meandering the length of Grassy Top,
falling off Sassafras
tumbling down Table Rock,
first claiming identity
at Big Spring, Sunfish, Galloway Branch,
Callahan, Rachael, Posey,
Willis, Emory, Oolenoy,
Devil's Fork, and Cold Spring.

And so it continues
past Cleveland and Marietta,
coming together at Pumpkintown and Dacusville,
serpentine centipede crawling past
Greenville and Piedmont,
Pelzer and Princeton.

After the fall line,

below the shoals,
the bluffs of Ridge Road
rise just enough
to turn Saluda left
and into lake,
gathering behind the dam
at Buzzard's Roost
before moving on to join Broad
to Congaree, Wateree to Santee,
and finally all to Ocean.

But here,
where the elbow makes an eddy
where anything, anyone,
floating down might catch
and climb out
and find a safe place
to call home,
where sounds of cicada,
plash of terrapin,
hover of buzzard,
all combine
at Mulberry Creek,
to form green water
near Greenwood,
what user of words
first declared this
a place where one
might seek refuge?

Crosses, you might expect,
graves, tombstones,
mysterious stacks
of rocky circles on the ground,
moonlight shining
through pine trees
everywhere at once.
Or was it just
the accident
of a church bus,
Soul's Harbor
scripted on its side,
breaking down
just here
where so much
seems possible.

Who Hasn't Contemplated Civil Disobedience Stuck Behind a Tractor Trailer Carrying Chickens to Dobson, NC

I mean we've all been there, right?
First offended by the stench of a thousand chickens
and their requisite shit, piss, cackle,
doomed pathetic feathers stuffed
between metal slats of a rolling henhouse,
chuffing them off to heaven-sounding Holly Farms
and cursing our luck that even though
every road around Dobson, NC,
is a country road as straight as it is narrow,
every time we try to pass we meet
a car coming the other way.
And so, we sit, stuffed in our own box
too tight to move, legs drawn up, arms bent,
back hunched over the wheel
until we start to feel more than a bit
sympathetic towards the horde
of *gallus domesticus* perched before us
certainly deserving better treatment
than this, and that's when our imaginations
begin to run a bit wild and we see ourselves
modern-day Thoreaus refusing our quiet
desperation and thinking for a moment
we might pull up alongside this slaughterhouse
on wheels, use an umbrella to wedge
the accelerator down, climb through the passenger
side window, swing ourselves onto the side
of the truck, sidle around to the back,
fling open the doors and scream
Fly free my fine-feathered friends.

But then, the vision continues
and their luminous white bodies
fall to asphalt one by one
and are crushed beneath the wheels of cars
whose drivers cheered us on
but moments ago, and so
we keep our seats, grip the wheel
of the minivan with two hands,
and try to stay between the lines.

Everything Is Made

Everything is made possible
by two most opposite of acts,
dividing and joining,
separating winter
from spring, light
from dark, even
when you know that one
contains plenty
of the other, combining
free and fall,
yours and mine,
open and window,
writer and desk,
revealing, expanding
here, now,
and all we've yet to know.

Teaching During the Pandemic

I put on my coat in my office
because it is cold here.
I find in a pocket 2 pens
one of them my favorite from a while back,
and in another a pair of reading glasses
the kind that fold up and fit
inside a case the size of a cigarette lighter
that flips open impressively
when you're bored or wanting to impress.

Last week it rained here,
in my office. I was sitting
in my chair when it happened.
I had just finished reading
my students' work and was working
on a poem about the Saluda River
and in my reverie I didn't understand
at first what was happening.
My head was in the poem
and I thought it was under water
and that it must have been
a damned good poem.
I never found out where
the rain had come from,
a busted pipe, probably a sprinkler,
but you can still see the water
stains in the ceiling tile
and a bit of water in the fixture
they never managed to get out.

I don't wear my mask here,
in my office, but I put it on
anytime I go to the bathroom,
classroom, coffee pot or copier,
or even just outside to enjoy the autumn
air as much as I can enjoy
the autumn air through my mask.
I've been reading Sandra Beasley here
and she fills me with a sense
of possibility of being a jukebox,
a college, God as a captor
of small birds, but mostly of being
a bumblebee, and I don't know why
she makes me think of bumblebees
except for maybe her name,
or the flitting flight and frequent
sting of her imagination.

People don't talk much through masks,
so so much goes unsaid.
They don't talk the way
they used to, mostly just grunts or nods,
as if by not speaking they might
spread the virus less and in that way
make things a little bit better,
so I guess it's just them trying
to be nice for once, and considerate
and keep us all a little safer,
but in the halls I hardly hear a sound
and the silence can be
more than a bit depressing.

My mask is black and so is my coat
and my shirt and I don't know what
that has to do with bees or Beasley
or rain or being cold.
I had hoped to get something done here
like putting my computer back together,
but instead I've only worked on this poem
and found three boxes that I can make use of
almost anywhere other than here.

Small Talk

When something's so small
the question's why bother at all.
The score of the game, the weather,
what stars have gotten together,
the condition that someone is in,
how this one or that one has been,
some meaningless random chitchat
almost anything to say of this or that.
They stumble in for their coffee
and leave what words they offer me
as if nothing's more meaningful to do,
but perhaps the true purpose is "I too."

I, too, have suffered.
I, too, have loved and lost.
I, too, wonder what it's all about.
I, too, hunger, pine,
long for answers, for something
above or beyond the abyss.
I, too, have heard the lack
of conviction, the unknowledge
in what people insist to be true.
I, too, search for the right words
to soften, assuage, allay fear.
I, too, have stepped
in my father's blood-filled bootprint.

I, too, am still trying
to try less, relax
into the fall, ask
for less definitive.
I, too, have stayed awake
in a darkened cell, afraid
to rise and venture out.
I, too, have wakened wet
with tears from dreams
of lost children, myself among them.
I, too, would trade places
with a corpse if not
for the uncertainty of dreams.
I, too, stumble forward
every day, as if I knew
the purpose, as if big answers
could be found in small talk.

The Possibility of Substance Beyond Reflection

I didn't see the V of geese fly overhead in the slate gray sky as I sat waiting for a reading in my Prius in front of the Royal Bean Coffee House & Gift Shop in Raleigh, NC.

What I saw was the V of geese presumably flying overhead in the slate gray sky reflected in the slate gray hood of the Honda CRV parked before me in front of the Royal Bean Coffee House & Gift Shop in Raleigh, NC.

And they took a long time to travel such a short distance, up one quarter panel, across one contoured crease, then the broad canvas of the hood's main body, down the other crease and onto the edge of the opposite quarter panel before

disappearing into the unreflective nothingness beyond, where even they had to question just how real they were or just how real they might have been.

What Words Are Worth

The creek speaks in words
that no one knows but everyone
feels say something about going
without going away.

What are words worth
if not to take us on a trip
and name the trip,
describe, characterize, analyze,
make meaning out of meaninglessness.

Last

I can't recount the number of times
I've been struck: father, stepfathers,
brother, grandmother, rivals, gangs,
abusers of others I've leapt to defend.
Yet even in the face of trauma,
and though the world itself can leave us
battered and bruised, we relish every sight
and sound, every sunrise, hawkflight,
smiling face, the music of words,
leaves kicked up ahead of our feet,
the way the dew springs from a clothesline
blurred by a morning mockingbird
leaping away, trusting to wings
to once again lift it into yellow air.

I can't recount the number of times
I've witnessed death: my grandfather
consumed by cancer, mother-in-law
imprisoned in the cell of her body by ALS,
my students falling off tractors, burning
in housefires, crushed in speeding cars.
Yet even in the face of tragedy,
we savor every drop of life,
cradle the cup, hold the taste
on our lips, tongues, back
of our throat for as long as we can.

In my dreams I have already died
a thousand deaths: falling, burning,
trapped under water, victim of anger
or random, pointless violence, alone,
helpless against my own slow suffering,
and I know that some unknowable day
one of these visions will come true.
Yet even in the face of our own
inevitable doom, we cling to every
second of every hour, every hour
of every day as if to something
precious, wanting only to make it
better, wanting always to make it,
whatever it may be to each of us,
last.

Survivors

My heroes are not those
who survive the horrors of war
anymore than they who survive

every day. Victors
of interior battles they hold
their demons at bay, keep

the gun in the drawer,
knife on the table,
pills in the bottle,

continue to fight the good fight
against daily injustice, uncertainty,
decades of being degraded

or told they don't matter,
they are less than, unworthy
of love, opportunity, fairness.

I love best those
who get up in the morning
no matter how bleak the prospect

of morning might be,
who stand up for themselves
or anyone else who needs it,

who continually, convincingly,
courageously,
    push things forward.

A Lot About Limas

Sometimes called Butter Beans
or Madagascars, Bushel Beans
or Hendersons, Moon Beans
or Dixies, like most legumes,
they're actually a seed,
and one of the oldest,
started in the Andes
some 7000 years ago,
which is why the capital of Peru
is named after them.

One of the first plants
exported to Europe.
The Spanish liked them so much
they built paella around them.

They can be dried, canned, or frozen,
boiled, sautéed, or steamed.

Some grow on bushes,
others on vines as long
as sixteen feet tied to poles
raised up and tented for easy picking.

My favorite vegetable as a boy
but not the white, soupy ones
my Granny covered with mayonnaise,

or the flat, baby ones
best with lots of black pepper.
I preferred the fat green ones
that came from the freezer.
I never knew the variety
and can't seem to find them anymore.
I called them fat lima beans,
so fat they'd pop in my mouth
like good shrimp or sugared cranberries.

Lima beans are not particularly political,
poetic, or parental,
but eaten raw, they are toxic,
and who can deny the eloquence
of a bowl of limas,
or the snuggle of peas in a pod.

Half-moon, fetal,
bottom-heavy apostrophe,
demitasse spoon, olive,
clam shell if split open,
eyes of Courage
or every anime girl ever drawn,
surprisingly symmetrical,
simple and satisfying.

My first car was a 10-year-old,
'72 green Nova with no backseat.
I called it the Lima Bean.

Despite having achieved little celebrity,
so much depends upon
lima beans
in a red serving bowl
beside the baked chicken.

Something Better

My friend asks if I don't
have something better to do
than mess with poems all day.

I ask him what
could be better than that?

*Who has time to write
of life*, he says, *while living it?*

*Who dare not
make such time*, I say,
*and by making,
save the life he's living*.

Assurances

It's lunchtime
and my daughter
home because of the virus
picks basil for her own bruschetta.
I know she's no Greta Thunburg,
and I would never ask her to be,
but she's not texting or tweeting
or googling where to find basil
in one ounce plastic packages
picked from someone else's
commercial garden halfway
around the world.
She knows where to find it
and how to cut the branch
above the lowest pair of leaves
and what to do with it
once she has it.
It's only basil you may say,
and no, she may never save
the world, but how many other
15 year olds know where and how,
and will take the time to harvest
and prepare on their own,
and I think it shows at the very least
that something her mother and I
have taught her has stuck
and it likely will again
some unfathomable number

of years from now
when someone we've yet to meet
calls her, Mother.

LONG
YELLOW

Long Yellow

Pen to lips,
eyes glossed over,
waiting for light
to change, there's no doubt
she's writing, like me,
while driving, notebook
balanced on one knee
just out of sight,
as if I might see
otherwise and know
the safest way to do
an unsafe thing.

I wonder how she manages
to keep it balanced,
stay between the lines.
I imagine she's writing
something important:
in a field of brown
ragged spent stems
something blue;
epiphany, apology,
merest observation:

> *pen to lips,*
> *eyes glossed over,*
> *waiting for light.*

Utilitarian

Who Shakespeare screwed and his iambic line
don't mean shit to the guy who rolls out at 5,
three thousand clucking chickens behind him
on their way to cackle their last at Holly Fucking Farms,
but even he needs and knows as much of beauty
as the next guy, warm cup of his neighbor
getting dressed for work, curve of thigh, mouth, brow;
sunrise over milepost 94 heading west on I40;
even the well-turned word hitting him harder
than any fist between the eyes ever did,
resonating some hundred miles after as he tries
to reconcile what he thought from what he heard
and make some useful sense of it all.

Poem for This Saturday's Apocalypse

Put your things in order.
Say your last *farewells*.
Make contrition, complete penance.
Say your prayers. Wait.

The signs are unmistakable:
earthquakes, Japanese tsunamis,
Mississippi floods, tornadoes
in the mountains of Tennessee.

The world ends again
this Saturday, the 12th time
in my lifetime. Of course,
the math might be faulty.

The numbers might not add up
and the words -- who can say
what they really say
until the end of days?

One thing only is certain:
one of these days
if we just keep guessing,
someone is bound to be right.

The Persistent Desire to Rise

Monday morning, Indian Garden,
a lone honeybee wrestles with anthers
of a prickly pear, extracting
what could be called a rough love,
stumbling over stamen as I have stumbled
four and a half miles down,
three thousand feet to achieve this sweet
breathing oasis among rock
without regard to heavy load
awaiting the climb back,
just as every other Monday morning
I enter a week full of expectation,
unconsidering the need for getting out
before turning, like rock, to abiding sand.

morning mirror
caught staring
into my own eyes

Aubade

At 5 o'clock, at 55,
I walk the mile on mid-November
streets, to the coffee shop I own
and open. Though all is dark,
I am not alone. I hear
footsteps rustle through leaves,
see the homeowner
roll his trash to the curb.

To the right on a porch lit spectral green
the remains of a woman sits,
crooked forward, legs crossed
at the knee, one foot rocking,
smoking a cigarette. She growls
a coarse *Good Morning*. A door
closes, the handed handle unseen.

On a parallel street, three figures
match me, walking fast,
voices just a mumble.
A pickup roars by,
bright lights intruding, prying.
Fearing no loss, I cut
through the unsafe alley
where people sleep in cars.

At the end the three ladies
of darkness finally catch me,
pass without a word,

continue their right angles
that slice the night apart.
I move forward,
knowing I'll see them again.

Sharing a Drink on My 55th Birthday

Sharing a drink on my 55th birthday,
my son, his tongue firmly planted
in his cheek, asks what advice I have
for those not yet as old as I,
and I, having had too much to drink,
miss his humor and tell him
always get up at 5
as if you don't want to miss
any part of any day you can manage.
Clean up your own mess
and don't clean up after those who won't.
Take the long way home,
hoping to see something new,
or something you don't
want to not see again.
Stay up late, drink in as much
of every day as you can.
Be drunk on life, on love, on trees,
on mountains, on spring,
on rivers that go the way
they know to go,
on words, on art, on dancing,
on poetry, on the newborn
fighting against nonexistence,
on night skies, on dreams, on mere minutes,
on the ocean that stretches beyond
what you ever imagined forever could be.
And when someone asks you
what advice you have, give them,
as you've given everyone and everything,
the best of what you have.

Isn't

My friend worries
of dying before
his time.

I say to him,
*If we live well
we'll all die*

*before our time.
Trying still
means there will always*

*be something left
unfinished.*

*Preparing to die
is no way to live.*

Maybe This

Maybe this is the last day of my life.
In case it's so I'll go now
to hug my wife and daughter.
I'll call my boys to tell them
I love them.
I'll read a few poems
and write one more.
Then I'll plant trees,
knees pressed into soil,
hair held back from my eyes,
sweat running down skin.
To remember roots
I'll give up on gloves,
tolerate dirt beneath nails,
feel earth pulling me home.
Maybe this, maybe tomorrow,
maybe next.

Keeping Pace

I'm slowing down,
not because I have to,
not because the joints
of my bones take longer to bend,
not because rising from bed
I've become like a crane slowly
unfolding and lifting from water,
but because I've learned
how much everything likes
to be touched gently, carefully,
slowly, because the good enough
job was never really
good enough, and more
was never better than good.

Making Amends

Autumn mornings you'll want to go into the yard
and put things right again. Wearing the old
shoes against the dew, taking advantage
of the sun's lethargic shining, you'll clip the stray
sprig of holly, pare back pyracantha, rake
leaves into piles. You'll brush off cobwebs from corners
of the house, clorox mildew beneath the gutters,
finally get the lawn edged the way you like it.
There won't be time for everything.
Old lilies might not get thinned,
the garage cleaned. Dead wood
will remain in the soffit, but each
redress will leave you that much closer
to rest and winter's closing in.

Not Going Gently

I know I've been walking
because my feet hurt.
I know I've been toting
because my shoulders ache.
I know I've been stooping
because my knees don't want to unbend.
I know I've been lifting
because it feels so good
when I twist my back
just enough for it to go *Pop!*
I know I've been living
because the people around me
all smile and seem to be happy.

Resistance

When the hand comes to rest
on my shoulder, I won't turn around,
or smile, or open my arms to it.
I won't willingly rise,
death's easy trick of levitation,
from the table laid out before me,
some meat I've prepared, some
prepared by others, the drink
poured by all who came before.

I'll finish the meal, savor the last
drop of wine and ask for more.
I'll argue the time is not right,
a mistake has been made. I'll call
names, scream embarrassing insults,
then dig fingers into the underside
of the chair, clamp teeth on anything
that comes near, slam my head
against their chin, the bridge of their nose.

Strong-armed angels, four at least,
will grip beneath each arm
and leg, pry at fingers
untwist feet from legs of chair,
and I'll use my words again to beg,
cajole, sing them into submission
for just one more second,
as if I had something
worth fighting to the death.

Only One

My wife won't let me speak
of being old, but I don't mind age
or dying. In all my favorite movies
the good guys always die, heroically,
of course, fighting to the very end,
seizing every moment, making
whatever has come before, worthwhile.
Like them, I think that must be
what matters most. And like them I think
if I'm busy enough, distracted by what
I am doing, doing for what I believe in,
for living, then it will be worthwhile
to the very end, and the end itself
might pass without me noticing at all.

Just

Just the opposite, he said,
of what he was born into,
but just the way
he'd have it be,
redeeming everything he was given,
the good, the bad,
the endless in between,
making, like Lear's Fool,
something out of nothing

 Scott Owens holds degrees from Ohio University, UNC Charlotte, and UNC Greensboro. He is Professor of Poetry at Lenoir Rhyne University, former editor of Wild Goose Poetry Review and Southern Poetry Review. He owns and operates Taste Full Beans Coffeehouse and Gallery and coordinates Poetry Hickory. He is the author of 16 collections of poetry and recipient of awards from the Academy of American Poets, the Pushcart Prize Anthology, the Next Generation/Indie Lit Awards, the NC Writers Network, the NC Poetry Society, and the Poetry Society of SC. He has been featured on The Writer's Almanac 7 times, and his articles about poetry have been featured frequently in Poet's Market.

Made in the USA
Monee, IL
16 May 2021